Going the Distance
My Life As A Special Olympian And Living With A Learning Disability

By Joshua Schwartz

D1605607

Edited by Andy Millman

ISBN: 9798489362498

Dedicated to my friend John Stovropoulos, my coach and friend Lew Goldstein, and my parents, Mike and Maria Schwartz.

Let me win. But if I cannot win, let me be brave in the attempt.

Special Olympics Oath

Chapter One

The Beginning

I am Joshua Schwartz. I was born August 17th, 1975, at Westlake Hospital in Melrose Park, Illinois, to parents Michael and Maria. I am the middle child of three. My brother Jamey is the oldest and my sister Elizabeth is the youngest.

I was diagnosed at seventeen months with a learning disability and when I was three years old I was placed into a special school named Kirk Developmental Training Center. I was never good at test-taking, even from the very start.

My family stayed in Wheeling, Illinois, until I turned six. When my sister, Elizabeth, was born, the condominium where we lived became too small for all of us. My grandma on my dad's side of the family owned the condominium. She'd gotten remarried to a man named Charlie. I didn't know him well but I know he was a doctor. They were living in a house in Glencoe, Illinois, and when Charlie died, my family and my grandma decided to switch places to live. My grandma took the condominium and we took the house.

I started grammar school at South school in Glencoe. I was held back a year because they did not think I was ready. In South School I had a friend name Scott, and we were good friends until I left South. I just lost touch with him. He had a dog name Sandy. I would go to his house from time to time.

I had another friend, Jim Molly, who was from Ireland. One time I went to a swimming party he and his mom threw at the condominium where they were living, which belonged to a friend of theirs. After I left South, he went back to his country.

I started fourth grade at Central Junior High School in 1984. That year I got an award for being the nicest person. I received a book called *The Day Jimmy's Boa Ate The Wash*. My special education class had a system

2

like a checkbook. If you made it to level three or four, you got to go on a big outing for the weekend at a special camp at George Williams College near Lake Geneva, Wisconsin.

Also at Central, they had a place for junior high kids to have fun and hang out called the Junior High Project. It was a spacious room with a TV and comfortable furniture, and it was located in the basement of the school. One of the staff, a woman named Joellen, had a pet monkey. I went over to her townhouse and got to play with the monkey. After a while of having the monkey, she realized she had to get rid of it because it was ruining her house.

In 6th grade, I started going to the Friday Night Mixed, a program run by North Suburban Special Recreation Association. I met my friend Melissa Slotar, who would later become one of my classmates in high school. In high school, Melissa and I would go to dances, prom, turnabout and homecoming together. She is now married to Jeremy Bleichman, who owns a health food store. Jeremy and Melissa met through a professional matchmaker. Melissa and I have stayed incredibly good friends.

I also met my friend John Stavropoulos at Friday Night Mixed. John was the one who told me about the C.I.T. (Counselor in Training) program. I became a C.I.T. and remained one until the program ended. I would get picked up at my house and then taken to the site where camp was held. In the morning we had school and had to plan out our lesson plans for the week. Then we would go to our groups and help supervise the campers. Each group would choose a camper of the day and the camp would choose a camper of the week. After the C.I.T program was over, I just became a camper for the summer. Being at day camp was fun. It gave me something to do so I was not stuck in the house all day doing nothing.

In 8th grade I got to go on the 8th grade trip. It was my first time on an airplane. We went to Washington

D.C. It was an exciting trip. One thing I loved was seeing

the mint where they make money.

Chapter 2

Glencoe Youth Services, The High School Drop-In Center

As I was growing up, I used to follow my brother around a lot, because he was older and cool and had cool friends. He was a really good baseball player and kept playing even after high school. I would go watch him play. Another thing I loved about my brother was that he played guitar and was awesome. He was in a band with his best friend, Chris Forte, who is now a professional musician and guitar instructor. Chris's family lived right by us and we used to see them often. His brother, Tommy, played baseball with my brother, and his sister Becky was my year in school and a student helper in Lew Goldstein's special education classes in high school. Lew would become my Special Olympics coach and one of my closest friends. Becky would eventually become a special education teacher.

My brother showed me lots of things, like how to ride a bike. He'd found an abandoned Schwinn girl's bike behind the junior high and that is the bike I learned to ride on. It was not easy at first, but I got the hang of it and now I can ride a bike perfectly.

The years went by and my brother moved to Colorado a few years after he finished high school. He recently moved to Texas. I never got a chance to visit him in Colorado. Maybe I'll get to see him in Texas. I miss my brother and the good times we had growing up.

Our house was across the street from a big field with tennis courts, baseball fields, and a small building that people used to use to warm up when they'd skate on the field during winter. One day my brother and I went across the street because there was a lady looking around the building. She told us that it was going to be the new home of Glencoe Youth Services.

Glencoe Youth Services was started in 1971 after a girl died from an overdose from an aerosol can. Some high school students, including some of her friends, asked the village board if they could start a youth center to get the kids off the streets and give them a place to hang out. The center moved around a lot until it found its permanent home in that little building, and it's still there today.

My brother got to go there before I did because he's older. In 1989, even though I was only in 8th grade, they started to let me go too. I met some very cool people there. I first met Carol Bickler, who was the Executive Director of Glencoe Youth Services. She grew up in Glenview, Illinois, and loved the Cubs. Then I met a special friend named Andy Millman. Andy was a Youth Worker at Glencoe Youth Services. He grew up in Wilmette, Illinois and went to New Trier West High School. We hit it off with music and movies and sports and he became my best friend. He moved to Milwaukee in 1991 to go to graduate school at Marquette University, but he came back in 1995 and took Carol's job after she moved to Memphis.

The youth center was for teens in New Trier Township who needed a place to get away and to relieve stress. The center had a TV, movies, video games, board games, and a pool table. Andy would play games with the kids and go on outings and just give kids time and a place away from home. The youth center helped a lot of kids who were having issues in their lives.

On the Fourth of July we used to sell glow-sticks at the Glencoe Fourth of July fireworks. During the day we would sell snow cones at their art fair. We were raising money for the youth center. We also ran game booths for kids at Pumpkin Day, which happened a couple weeks before Halloween every year.

One important thing the youth center did was organize concerts with the Winnetka Youth Organization in Winnetka. The Winnetka Youth Organization, which everyone called The Yo, was in the basement of the Winnetka Community Center. The center was run by Mary Ellen Spicer. I met her through Andy. We are all

9

still good friends. My brother and his friend Chris had a band that played there. They were first called White Frost and later changed their name to Soul Farmer.

I started New Trier High School in Winnetka, Illinois, in 1990. The next four years would be the best of my life. New Trier was much bigger than Central School, and it was hard at first to find my way around, but I would just ask for help and eventually would get used to it. My freshman year I had class on the 4th floor and then had to go all the way downstairs to the basement every single day.

I took the public bus to school, which cost me $1.75. I saw my friend John after all those years, and one day in class he explained that the medals he was wearing were from Special Olympics. My teacher, Ludmilla Covin, asked if I would like to join the Special Olympics team. I said yes, of course, and that is where I met Lew Goldstein, the head coach, and Terry Witt, the assistant coach. I was

15 when I started, and I have been in it ever since and never looked back.

Lew and I have known each other over thirty years and are very close friends. He started teaching at New Trier high school in 1979 as the E.M.H, or Educable Mentally Handicapped, teacher. He got to do what he wanted except for hiring teachers. Also in 1979, he brought Special Olympics to New Trier, and they loved it and kept it ever since. One person I met on my team was Shawn Anthony Robinson. Shawn was having trouble in school and they thought becoming a mentor and student helper would help him stay out of trouble. He has since graduated from new Trier and now has a Ph.D. He is currently the Senior Research Associate at the Wisconsin's Equity and Inclusion Laboratory. He is also married with two kids and has written two books: *Doctor Dyslexia Dude!* and *Dr. Dyslexia Dude! and the Battle for Resilience* about his struggles. When he went to college, he was reading at a 3rd grade level. That is where he found out he has

Dyslexia. He inspired me to write my book that you are reading. Because if he could do it, so can I.

I graduated high school in 1994. Things were changing fast. For the first time since I could remember, I was no longer in school. Fortunately, Lew let us continue with Special Olympics, and I did. Another big change after high school was not going to the youth center as much, since it was for high school kids. Carol, and later Andy, would let me come in and help around the center. I was kind of a volunteer and Andy often said that I knew the place better than anybody. Luckily, there was a new program for people who had graduated high school and still wanted to do some of the same things we did at the youth center.

The Young Adult Program, or YAP, was held every Tuesday night from 6 to 9 at the Glencoe Youth Services' building. Don Miner, who worked at a nonprofit organization called Haven, was the very first leader of YAP. Don was an awesome friend. I met him because he used to come to my high school and talk with kids as part of his job. At first the program was focused on recent high school graduates. Soon it became an advocate and program for adults with disabilities.

After Don left, a young woman named Jenny Goodman took over. She ran the program until Haven decided to stop sponsoring the program. Then the Josselyn Center took over until they decided to stop sponsoring us. For a very short time Center for Enriched Living ran it but then they dropped it too.

I took it upon myself to go to the New Trier Township to talk to the board to ask if they would support us. Brian Leverenz, the Community Services Administrator, said to come back Monday and we will go from there. We had a meeting with some of the participants and my best friend Andy. After a while they just said have Glencoe Youth Services run it and they did. I only wanted three people to run it, because they were the only ones I trusted; my friends Ken Clayborne, Don, and Andy.

Andy was really happy to take the job and it was like old times, the two of us back in the youth center together. He said it was one of the best jobs he ever had. My family had recently sold our house in Glencoe and moved to Grayslake, which is about twenty-five miles from Glencoe. Even though I now had to find ways to get there, I was there almost every Tuesday night. I missed the days when I could just walk across the street to go there, but things have a way of changing even if you don't want them to.

Andy kept working there until he moved to Madison, Wisconsin, in 2014 to be with his girlfriend. I deeply miss Andy and that is when I stopped going to the program. Andy and I always stay connected. I always call him and he always calls me. We have a good friendship, even though we are farther apart than we would like to be.

Chapter 3
Living with a Learning disability

Living with a disability can limit you. People might tell you all the things you cannot do. But sometimes we don't know what we can do until we try to do it. My mom noticed I was struggling to learn when I was very young. She had my IQ checked and it was below normal, and that's when she enrolled me in that special program at Kirk Developmental Training Center. I'm lucky that my mom found a place that would help me learn how to learn.

My disability consists of me learning slower than others. When things go too fast, I can get confused. Some things are harder for me to learn than other things. Math was hard for me, especially things like times tables. I should have been in Lew's math class in high school, but we did not know I needed that much help in that area.

I had some surprisingly good teachers who knew how to teach me. I needed to learn in a smaller class. If a class was too big, I could not function properly. If I had one on one time with a teacher, it was easier for me to learn. For example, I was put into a special science class with a bunch of disruptive kids, and I got a C in the class. The next year I took the same class without the disruptive kids and I got a B +.

I was able to study the same subjects that other kids studied in high school, though some of my classes focused on helping kids with learning disabilities. I took a Spanish class and still remember some of the words, but I can't speak a full sentence in Spanish.

I did very well in many classes. During junior year, every student was required to write a "Junior Theme." It was the longest paper we would write in high school, and the longest thing I'd ever written until the book you are now reading. Reading comes easy to me, and if I don't understand what I'm reading, I'll ask for help. I picked Walter Ellis Disney for my Junior Theme topic. I read a lot about him and enjoyed it. Then I wrote up the paper on him. A bunch of people read it, and I got all A's. I am glad I had the teachers I did because they knew how to teach me, and it made me feel like I belonged.

I used to see a speech therapist to help me with my letters and writing. I had trouble with "w" and "r." I would say words with the letters and mix them up. My "w" would sound like an "r," and vice versa. I now can say words more clearly. I also saw another speech therapist in Glenview, Illinois, to help me with my memory and other stuff.

Some classes were challenging. I took a special driver's education class in high school because it was required to graduate. I barely passed, but because of my learning disability, the school said I shouldn't drive. I didn't really mind, because I was already getting good at taking buses. At some point after the class ended, I was talking about how I would never be able to drive. Andy told me that it was okay not to drive, but he wanted to show me that I could do it. We went in his car to a hotel parking lot and then he told me to get behind the wheel and drive around, while he sat next to me and gave me tips. I did better than I remembered doing in class.

I still don't drive, but I've gotten really good at reading bus and train schedules and figuring out how to get to places. If I need help, I have people who support me. Lew, my head coach, takes me to the train on Wednesdays and Thursdays to go home so I can still be in Special Olympics and a Life Skills program that is run by Northwestern students for our Special Olympics team.

Learning disabilities affect more than school work. When someone asks me to do something, I need it to be explained a little differently than others would. Having instructions repeated a couple times helps me. My attention span is also noticeably short. I can only concentrate for so long. I have trouble managing money. It is hard to save money when you do not make a lot. I am trying to save and do better, but things are expensive.

Fortunately, people are always there to help me learn if I need it. I just know I have to ask.

Many of my friends have learning disabilities, and some have physical disabilities like spina bifida or cerebral palsy. My friend Jake Joehl is blind, and so is his brother Sam and sister Claudia. Claudia is on our Special Olympics team. She competes in the tennis ball throw and a rope race, where she uses the rope to guide her. The rope is fifty-feet long. Claudia holds a baton that slides along the rope as she races. I met Jake in 1984 and we have been friends ever since. Jake and I went to the same speech therapist. Every year the speech therapist would take us to the circus. Jake wore headphones to listen to an announcer describe what was happening on the stage.

I love helping others. Even though I am learning disabled, I can still help others with stuff like reading, the computer, and photography, just to name a few. I am always showing my coach Lew how to use his flip phone and the computer since it is hard for him. It makes me feel special that I can do that while having a learning disability. He's taught me a lot, but I've taught him a few things too. One day I would like to build a desktop computer. I have never done that, but I think it would be one of my greatest achievements.

I started photography during my freshman year of high school. A few years later, I met my friend Ken Clayborne through the Young Adult Program, where he would help out. Ken is an awesome photographer and has taught me a lot. I loved going over to Ken's house because his family was so nice. They would always offer me something to eat. They have since moved from Glencoe to Augusta, Georgia. I deeply miss Ken. He is and always will be a great friend.

Helping others gives me a sense of gratitude. I'm thankful that even though I am limited, I can still do things to help others. I like it when people ask me for help, because they know I have a certain ability that can help them. I am okay with having a learning disability, because that is how God made me, and it shows who I am and what I can do.

Chapter 4

How I Prepare for Special Olympics

The two people probably most responsible for creating Special Olympics were Eunice Kennedy Shriver and Anne Burke. Anne Burke was working with the Chicago Park District when she got the idea to hold an Olympics-style competition for people with disabilities. Eunice Kennedy Shriver, sister of John F. Kennedy, had been running a camp at her house for kids with intellectual and physical disabilities. Her sister Rosemary was born with an intellectual disability, and many people think that's why Eunice became interested in helping people with disabilities. Eunice liked Anne's idea and asked her to include athletes from all over the country, which she agreed to do. Five years after Eunice opened her camp, the very first Special Olympics was held at Soldier Field in Chicago in 1968. Approximately 1000 athletes from the U.S. and Canada competed. Today it is estimated that over five million people participate in Special Olympics every year.

The one person responsible for bringing Special Olympics to my high school is my coach, Lew Goldstein. Lew learned about Special Olympics from his cousin, who attended the second competition, held in 1969. Lew created a Special Olympics team at the school he was working at in Chicago. When he got to New Trier, he did the same thing. Lew also created a unique program where students would help in the classroom and at Special Olympics practices.

One of those student helpers was Emily Dutterer. Emily helped at our practices and even went with us to the state games. She enjoyed helping people so much that she became a special education teacher. Then she joined the Peace Corps. And now, for the past ten years, she's been working for Special Olympics.

My Special Olympics team is called North Shore Special Olympics. Most of my teammates went to New

Trier High School like I did, but our team is open to anyone. We have athletes that went to other schools and found out about our team and joined up. We are a unique team because we are not affiliated with any one school or organization.

Lew has an assistant coach named Terry Witt who helps him a lot. I met Terry in the spring of 1991 through my Special Olympics practices. Terry is one of the smartest people I have ever met. He could be a world-class astronomer and mathematician. He is that smart. Terry is exceptionally good at helping us achieve our goals.

I met two other special people on the team around that time: Mike Mensching and Merrill Kalin. Mike was a great all-around athlete and helped coach youth football. He loved sports, especially the Cubs, and had a very large baseball card collection, which he would bring over to Glencoe Youth Services. He competed in the softball throw and the running relay on our team. Merrill was the shot putter on our team. He was probably the only one who could lift the shot put! He was also a good cook and hosted a cooking show on television. The program was produced with the help of an organization called Little City, which is where Merrill lived. You can still see episodes of the show on YouTube.

Sadly, both Mike and Merrill have passed away. Merrill died in 2008, and Michael died in 2017. Both of their obituaries mentioned their participation in Special Olympics. Lew spoke at Merrill's funeral and talked about Merrill as a student and as an athlete, and as a kind human being. The seats were filled with his teammates and former classmates. Lew and the team are always there when times are difficult.

Another important member of our team is Brian Brandt, who's an assistant coach. Brian used to be the President of the Glencoe Park District Board, and he also was on the board of directors at the youth center. Brian discovered our team because he used to help out at the Young Adult Program, and Andy thought that he and

Lew should meet each other. Now Brian and Lew are great friends. Brian is awesome. He has two daughters, Caitlin and Ashley. Caitlin also used to help out at the Young Adult Program. Brian is a wonderful coach and friend.

Our practices begin the third Thursday of February. We meet at 6:30 PM at New Trier. If the weather permits, we might go outside to practice, but that wouldn't be until spring time. We start by stretching and warming up so we don't pull a muscle. Then we go to the long jump. Once you've done the long jump, you go over to Terry and start your main event. My teammates who have a physical disability and can't do the long jump wait for their main event practice. After the long jump, we get ready for our main event. I do the 100-meter run.

One of the lessons I've learned in Special Olympics is to *go the distance*. At first, this lesson meant to not slow down or stop before I reached the finish line of a race. I need to keep pushing and trying until the very end. But then I realized that going the distance also meant not giving up on things. If I'm competing in a new sport, it might be difficult at first, but I need to keep practicing and learning, or else I'll never even know what I'll be able to do.

If we have time, we do the 4 x 100 running relay. Others start their walking relays. There are only two people on the team who compete in the 400-meter race walk. One of those people is my friend John Stavropoulos. John is very fast and does well in the event. The other person, though, is a champion, and the fastest walker I've ever seen.

Gary Berliant is an amazing athlete and a joy to watch when he race walks. Race walking is more difficult than it looks. Walkers must keep one foot in contact with the ground at all times. If you're jogging or running, there will be times when both feet will be off the ground. Gary is so fast that some helpers have to jog just to keep up with him. In 2006 he went to Ames, Iowa to compete in the very first Special Olympics National Games, and he became a 3-time walking champion.

Back in 6th grade, when I was going to day camp, I met my good friend Tom Balzer. Tom is also on my team. He is awesome and fun to hang out with. Tom competes in basketball, Bocce Ball, and track and field with my team, and volleyball and softball with the North Suburban Special Recreation Association (NSSRA) team. Tom is an exceptionally talented volleyball player. In 2003, Tom went to the international Special Olympic games in Dublin, Ireland, where his NSSRA team beat a top team from Texas and won the gold medal for volleyball.

After we are done practicing, we all go out to dinner together. We normally go to Homer's Ice Cream in Wilmette. Homer's is famous for their ice cream but they serve meals, too. Homer's was started in 1935 and they still use the original recipes for making their ice cream. Hanging out together after practice allows us to socialize with our teammates, coaches, parents, and helpers.

I will continue in Special Olympics for as long as I can or until my coach retires. Special Olympics has allowed me to make friends and feel included. It is the one thing I look forward to every year because it is the most fun thing I do every year.

Chapter 5

What Special Olympics Means to Me

Special Olympics gives me the opportunity to show the world what I can do, rather than what I cannot do. I have won tons of medals. I started with Special Olympics in the spring of 1991 with my head coach Lew. He has taught me a lot through the years, and he is the best coach I have ever had.

I normally compete in the 100-meter dash, the long jump, and the running relay. The Special Olympics regional games are held the third week in May on Saturday and Sunday. Sometimes it will rain and the competition might be postponed or cancelled and rescheduled. If you get a gold medal in any of your sports, you get to go downstate to Normal, Illinois, to compete in the summer state games at Illinois State University. Those games are held the third weekend in June.

Our team leaves for Illinois State at 7:30 on Friday morning. Since I live too far away, I will sleep over at Lew's house and help him get ready for the trip. Lew will have a team packet with all the information we'll need for the games. We take a coach bus downstate. The bus has comfortable seats and TVs to watch movies. The ride takes about two and a half hours.

When we get to the campus, we get our room assignments. Lew gives us the keys to our dorm rooms, and we go put our stuff away. If we lose our key, there's a $50 charge to replace it. We'll all have lunch together while our teammate Gary Berliant competes in his race walking event.

June in central Illinois can be very hot and humid, so we need to be careful not to overdo it. There are lots of activities to do and things to see. Friday night starts everything off in a very special way with the opening ceremonies to start the summer state games.

Most of us have our events on Saturday and Sunday. On Saturday, we must be up by 6 a.m. to have breakfast and then get ready for our events, and we all must wear our uniforms. We can go off with a coach or friend if Lew knows where we are. No matter what we might be doing during the day, we have to be at our event a half hour early, or else we can be disqualified. I have seen people get disqualified and it makes me sad to think that someone put in all that work and had to miss competing because they showed up late to their event. There are responsibilities that come with being an athlete, and you have to take them seriously.

Because I like photography, I have become the team photographer. I take lots of pictures over the weekend and during our practices, and I'll put together a DVD slide show, which everyone seems to like. After a long day of competition on Saturday, we go to a dance with over 5,000 other athletes. After the dance, if we have time, we'll have a pizza party to celebrate our accomplishments.

Sunday is another busy day. First, we must pack and put our stuff on the bus. Then we head over to the track to get ready for the relay events, which are team events. Once the games are over, it's back to the bus and our ride back to Winnetka. We are all exhausted, but happy, from the great, fun-filled weekend. Even though the games are over, it doesn't mean our time together is over.

Lew schedules many activities for our team even when we're not practicing for the summer games. He worked with students from Northwestern University, which is close by, to start a Life Skills program. Lew and members of our team meet the Northwestern students at their student union, where we have dinner together. After dinner, we go to a meeting room and discuss subjects such as transportation, budgeting, and health.

Every year we have a Special Olympics team banquet at the Renaissance Hotel in Northbrook. Lew schedules the banquet to take place after the Regional Games and before the State Games. The banquet starts at 6:30 p.m. and goes to about 10 p.m., and it costs about $26 per person for athletes and any guests they bring. Over one hundred people usually attend, and sometimes there have been over two hundred. Terry will make name tags with seat assignments. Each table has ten people around it, and there are mixes of athletes, families and friends all around the ballroom. Everyone is dressed up to celebrate our accomplishments.

After dinner, Lew will start the program. He'll thank everyone for supporting the team and attending the banquet. He'll talk about how the team has done and the excitement he has for those of us who will be going downstate to compete at the State Games. He'll also call us up, one by one, and present us with any medals we won at the Regional Games. After Lew is done, the music and dancing will start. We have a wonderful time.

One of the other activities Lew organizes for the team is Bocce Ball. During October, before we begin training for Regional Games, we meet at our old high school for Bocce. If you've never played, Bocce Ball is a type of lawn bowling. You have a white cue ball that you roll down the court and you try to get all your other balls closer than your opponent's. Whoever's ball is closest gets a point per ball. The first person to get twelve points or is winning after half an hour wins the match.

Believe it or not, we once got to play Bocce Ball on Soldier Field, the home of the Chicago Bears. In 1968, the first ever Special Olympic Games were held at Soldier Field. On the 50th anniversary of the first games, a celebration was held back where it started, and we were thrilled to be a part of it. Playing Bocce Ball in Soldier Field, surrounded by my teammates and other athletes, was magical and something I'll never forget.

Special Olympics has given me so many wonderful memories. In addition to track and field and Bocce Ball, I've also competed in bowling, basketball and floor hockey. Our floor hockey team once went to Ann Arbor, Michigan, to compete in a tournament. It was so much fun. We used to have enough athletes to form two basketball teams and both teams would compete in a tournament. Maybe our teams were too good, because we now have trouble finding any that want to play us. I also like bowling, and members of our team compete in that, too. If you win a gold medal in the first round, you go to the second round. If you win a gold in the second round, you go to Peoria to compete in the State Games.

Winning a gold medal is the best feeling in the world. It makes me happy to show what I did in my events. I bring those medals home to show people who could not be there how I did.

It also makes me very happy to see my friends earn gold medals or just do as best as they can do. There are diverse types of people with disabilities. Some disabilities are big, some are small, some are mental, and some are physical. We are all in this together. To see people in wheelchairs and others walk with a walker or crutches, and to see them win or try their best is just the best thing in life. My team has all types of disabilities, and it is amazing to see what they can accomplish. I love every one of them.

Chapter 6

My Work

I got my first job in high school, and it was actually in my high school. I did office work in the attendance office during school hours. I also helped a woman named Barbara Rubens run a food stand in the student lounge. She volunteered with my Special Olympics team and was wonderful. Also during high school, I got a job at the local Walgreen's. I stocked shelves there once a week from 1991 to 1992. It was not enough hours for me to make a living, otherwise I might still be working there. It was not a bad job, just not enough hours.

Then I got a job bagging groceries and stocking shelves at The Grand Food Center in Winnetka, which was in the film *Home Alone*. In 1995, I started working at a different grocery store named Dominick's. I worked there for eighteen years, the longest I've worked at any one job. I would bag groceries, get carts, and clean the store. I also would put items people did not want back on the shelves. There are some tricks to being a good bagger. The first thing I would do is look at the customer and their order to see how many bags they would need. I would ask how they wanted their food packed, if they wanted paper or plastic bags, and if I should double any of the bags.

I worked with a lot of good people at Dominick's. The Safeway chain bought out Dominick's in 1998. I continued working there, and in 2001, when my family moved to Grayslake, Illinois, I transferred to a Dominick's out there. On 21st, 2014, all the Dominick's stores were closed down. I lost my job after eighteen years.

It was difficult to let go of my job, but I had no choice. I filed for unemployment, which I received until I got a job at Mariano's Fresh Market, another grocery store, two months later. I stayed with Mariano's for two years. On May 3rd, 2016, I started a new job at Always Enterprise Inc., a local cleaning contractor, where I am still working six years later.

James Franz, my boss at Always Enterprise Inc., is amazing. James is a self-taught businessman who started this business. He's also very nice. He picks me up and takes me home when we work. My position there is porter. We clean various places. The main places I clean are Bass Pro Shop and Cabela's. We sweep and wash floors, dust, get garbage, and make sure the floors are safe. I sweep the store and then I use a floor scrubber to wash the floors at Cabela's. When a floor needs a clean-up, you always must bring a "Wet Floor" floor sign and place it for safety. We also clean the bathrooms. My boss sometimes may need my help to clean other places too. It makes a big difference who you work with, and I'm glad I get to work with James.

Chapter 7

My Family

My brother, sister and I are all grown up now. Jamey lives in Texas, and my sister lives in a suburb about an hour and a half away from where I live with my mom and dad. She is married and has two children: my niece Kaylee, who was born in 2013, and nephew Nick, who was born in 2007. My sister is doing a wonderful job as a mother. She is very kind and loving. I love my niece and nephew and was so excited when they were added to our family.

My mom was born in Seattle, Washington. Her father, Gerald Ramage, was stationed in Alaska during World War II. The family lived in Seattle because it was close to my grandfather. After he left the service, the family moved to Chicago, which is where my mom was raised. She attended Calvin Park High School.

My dad was born in Evanston, Illinois, and attended Evanston High School. He met my mom in the Old Town neighborhood of Chicago in 1966. They were introduced by friends. In January, 1970, they moved to San Francisco. They moved back to the Chicago area a couple years later, and that is where my brother was born.

I have three aunts, two uncles, and lots of cousins. My uncle Samuel Ramage was sick for a while, but he's doing much better now. When I was younger he took me to see these big cars with very loud engines race down a dirt track. It was awesome. He also showed me his record player that could play 45's and 33's. I remember it sounding so great. He is married to Kathy Jean, and they have a son of their own, named David. David is married and has a child named Fox.

My aunt Barbie Ramage passed away a long time ago. I miss her a lot. She was a sweetheart. Barbie had one child, Melissa. She is the oldest of all the cousins. Melissa works at a restaurant. She once worked at a restaurant where some friends and I would go, and I would get to see her. My aunt Becky Tuttle has spina bifida and must be in a wheelchair, but she uses a scooter to get around. She has a loving husband named George. My aunt Kathy Moronic has two kids, Jackie and Victoria, whom we call Vicky. Vicky is the oldest and has two kids of her own, Isaac and Amber. Jackie is very talented. She has a wonderful singing voice and can play the flute beautifully. She's currently going for her PhD. When I was young my Aunt Kathy and her daughter Vicky took me to a religious camp in Wisconsin and another in Tennessee. Those were good times.

My mom's parents eventually moved back to Kentucky, which is where they were from. I loved visiting them there and seeing their beautiful home. I especially liked seeing my uncle Matt. He is musical, like my brother. Uncle Matt is a great drummer. Like my Uncle Sammy, Uncle Matt was also sick for a while, but he's also better now.

My grandfather Gerald Ramage passed away from an aneurysm in 1992, right before his birthday. His wife, my Grandmother Georgia Ramage, died in 2006 from old age. I deeply miss them. They were the best grandparents I could ever have.

On my dad's side of the family, there were two children: my dad and my aunt Sharon Bender. Sharon has three children: my cousins Elena, Isaac and Mitch. What is interesting is that my grandmother, Ann, knew my coach, Lew. They used to have brunch together with a mutual friend before Lew and I ever met. My grandmother told him that she had grandchildren that would be going to the high school where he was teaching. So, Lew heard about me before ever meeting me. My grandmother Ann has since passed away. I never knew my dad's father that well, and he has also passed away.

Animals have always been a big and important part of our family. One summer we were visiting my mom's family in Kentucky. Her mom's sister, Louise Utley, had puppies that they were trying to find homes for. Even though my dad said no, we took a puppy anyway. We named him Spike and he lived to be sixteen years old. Spike and I spent so much time together, walking around Glencoe and hanging out at the house. I even used to take him to the youth center, where he also liked to hang out.

After Spike died, we got a dog named Rosie, who was an American Eskimo. She lived until she was fifteen. After she died, we got Maggie, who is still with us. Maggie is a Red Bone Coonhoud. As I write this, in 2021, she is two years old.

We've had a few cats, too. My cat Candy had a few kittens. We kept one and my sister named him Felix, because he looked like Felix the Cat. We also had a cat named Fanny, who was given to us by my grandparents. There was another cat we named Monica, who was awesome. Right now we have a cat named Lulu, who was given to us by my Aunt Kathy.

I'm currently working with an organization that is trying to help me find affordable housing and government benefits. I would like to try living on my own. If I do, I'd also like to have an animal or two with me.

Chapter 8

My Hobbies

In my spare time when I'm not competing or practicing for Special Olympics, I enjoy doing different types of things. One activity I like is riding my bike. It's been a long time since my brother taught me how to ride a bike and I've ridden many, many miles since then. Going on long bike rides helps me relax and clear my mind. It's also one of the ways I get around.

I've always enjoyed being around animals. In addition to dogs and cats, I've also had tropical fish. I also like seeing wild animals. Many squirrels lived around my house in Glencoe and in the park across the street. One day I noticed a squirrel by the trash container outside the youth center. Something seemed wrong. When I looked closely, I saw its head was stuck in a yogurt container. I was able to follow the squirrel around and eventually pull the container off his head. Andy was amazed by this and said that squirrel would always be grateful to me.

My favorite thing in the world is music. I don't think I can live without music. When I'm out and about, I have to have my headphones. When I was a kid, I used to have a boombox that I would bring around. Andy and I like a lot of the same music. Our favorite band, which became Carol's favorite band (except for maybe the Beatles), is R.E.M. After Carol moved to Memphis, she started working at a store that was partly owned by one of R.E.M.'s managers. She was able to get backstage passes for her, me and Andy to go see R.E.M. at the Rosemont Horizon outside Chicago. She told Andy what she was doing, but neither of them told me. Andy said that we were meeting her for dinner. He parked a few blocks away from the Rosemont Horizon, so I didn't know we were going there. He told us that Carol had made dinner reservations for us. When we met her, she said, "Here are your reservations." She handed me an envelope and there were two backstage passes for me and for Andy. I could hardly believe we were about to go see my favorite band perform, and then I couldn't believe it when we were standing back stage after the show and I got to see Peter Buck, the R.E.M. guitarist, walking around with his kids.

If I had known I was about to see R.E.M., and if the band would have permitted it, I would have brought my camera. I've been interested in photography since I was a kid. My friend Ken is a great photographer and he's taught me a lot about it. I take all kinds of pictures. I enjoy working on the computer and nowadays people often use their computers to edit their pictures. Sometimes I take the train to Chicago just to take pictures. There are so many things to see there. I also like taking portraits and I hope to do that for a living one day.

My head coach, Lew, is a fantastic artist. He studied medical drawing in college. He collects etchings and has taught me about those. For those who don't know what an etching is, the artist takes a special tool and etches a drawing onto a copper plate. The drawing should be done backwards, because eventually it will be stamped onto paper. Black ink is poured into the grooves and then is left to dry for a little while. Finally, this is stamped onto paper which is run through a printing press. How these guys do it is amazing. I have some etchings that were made as far back as the 1800s. Lew's collection of etchings is huge, and sometimes we'll trade with one another.

I also like movies a lot. My favorite is the *Back to the Future* trilogy. The star of those movies, Michael J. Fox, is my favorite actor. A neat thing is that on the *Family Ties* TV show, Michael J. Fox's dad was played by Michael Gross, who went to school with my mother. Another good movie is *Groundhog Day*. The youth center once hosted an outdoor movie and showed *Groundhog Day*. The actress who played the piano teacher in the movie actually came and spoke. It was awesome.

I met another person connected to a movie. He didn't act in it or write it or direct it, but he was the inspiration for it. Homer Hickam wrote the book *Rocket Boys* about his childhood in Coalwood, West Virginia, and his dream of becoming a rocket scientist. He and his friends built model rockets and eventually won a National Science Fair gold medal. The movie *October Sky* is based on his book. I recently learned that if you take all the letters in *Rocket Boys* and rearrange them, you can spell *October Sky*. Lew had heard about the movie and we went to see it. Then he found out that the Homer Hickam would be speaking at Northwestern University, and we went to see him. After the talk, we bought copies of his book and waited in line to meet him and have him sign the book.

I like to study history, and so I enjoy many documentaries, especially ones by Ken Burns. He's made many great movies about topics such as jazz, the civil war, and the national parks. I hope to go to some of the national parks and spend a lot of time there taking pictures. Maybe I could put together a book of those pictures or sell some. My favorite film of his, and my favorite documentary, is *Baseball*. I really like sports. My favorite team is the Chicago Cubs. I'm a Cubs fan for life, but I also like the White Sox, which is parents' favorite team.

Geoffrey Baer is not as well-known as Ken Burns, but people around Chicago might know him because he hosts many films about Chicago. He's in films about Chicago's Loop, lakefront, and North Shore, where I lived. The North Shore refers to the suburbs north of Chicago that run along Lake Michigan.

When I lived in Glencoe, I was about four blocks away from Lake Michigan. I loved taking long walks on the beach and just looking at the lake. There's an overlook at Glencoe Beach, and a scene from *Ferris Bueller's Day Off* was filmed there. It's a great spot to watch the sun rise over the lake. The lake is also fun for swimming, which I also like to do.

There is one new hobby I have that I didn't know I'd enjoy as much as I do. It's writing. This has been such a fun exercise that I'm already thinking about writing another book. Maybe if this book does well I'll write a kid's book.

I've learned to never take life for granted. I try to always remember what life is about.

There is so much beauty all around us. There are things to do and see no matter where you live. Sometimes you just need to explore.

Chapter 9

Final Thoughts

I wrote this book to show how my disability affects me and hopefully to help you with your own way of learning. Everybody learns differently. No two people are alike, and everybody learns in their own way. For me, learning in a smaller class size helped a lot. Hearing instructions repeated helped a lot. I didn't know this right away. I had to learn how I learn.

Think about how you learn best. Whatever helps you learn is okay, because that is who you are, and nobody can take that away from you. Don't try to do it the way everybody else does. Do it the way that works for you. If you need help, ask for help. Never worry about what others think of you, because you'll never get far if you do.

Special Olympics taught me that I can do things I thought I could not do. The confidence I developed in

Special Olympics helped me try things outside of Special Olympics. I found there are lots of things I can do and learn, even if my learning style is different than others' learning styles. I've learned how important it is to never give up and to always keep trying. There are usually people around to help if you ask for it. I've also learned how rewarding it is to offer my help to others who might need it.

There are things we learn on our own, but there are many more things we learn with someone's help. I think about the activities I enjoy – many of them are described in this book – and I think about the people who helped me learn them. My brother taught me how to ride a bike; my friend Ken taught me about photography; my coach Lew introduced me to etchings. A learning disability doesn't stop me from learning. I'm grateful to all those people in my life who never stopped teaching me.

I intend to keep learning, and I hope you do, too. There's nothing to lose by trying, and lots to be gained.

Just like in life, there might be many obstacles to go through. No one said life would be easy. It's okay if you get upset or frustrated. Just slow down and take a deep breath and relax and think about what you are trying to do. When I'm having difficulty, I get up and go for a walk or call a friend or listen to music. That's what helps me relax and clear my mind. Then later I can go back and continue with what I was doing.

All we can do is live our lives to the best of our abilities and be the people we were meant to be. Be the best YOU that you know how to be. Go the distance. It's okay if you stumble at first. It's not about how your start the race, it's about how you finish it.

As I get older, I look to the future and what is to come. The only thing I know for certain is that there will be more to learn.

I appreciate you taking the time to read my book. Writing it was one of those things I wasn't sure I could do, but now I do. And now it's your turn. Go learn something new and do something that maybe no one thought you'd ever do. You just might surprise yourself, and everyone else.

Let's hope we all have great things to come.

Joshua Schwartz grew up in Glencoe, Illinois and graduated from New Trier High School. This is his first book. He can be contacted at Josher256@gmail.com.